HAPPY HALLOWEEN

Jessica Mazurkiewicz

3-D GLASSES INSIDE!

Dover Publications, Inc.
Mineola, New York

Note

Add some tricks and treats to the Halloween season with this 3-D coloring book featuring full-page patterns created from traditional imagery. Highlights include witches on broomsticks, haunted houses, vampires, Halloween candy, black cats, goblins, ghouls, and more! Each pattern is enclosed inside a detailed border for a finished look. The 30 black-and-white images created by artist Jessica Mazurkiewicz will make a distinctive holiday project for colorists of all ages. Read the intstructions on the inside covers for a guide to 3-D coloring. Then, select your choice of coloring media to add your own unique touch to these festive holiday designs, and finally, put on the 3-D glasses to see the pictures leap right off the page!

Bibliographical Note

3-D Coloring Book—Happy Halloween is a new work, first published by Dover Publications, Inc., in 2011.

International Standard Book Number

ISBN-13: 978-0-486-48411-2
ISBN-10: 0-486-48411-4

Manufactured in the United States by Courier Corporation
48411403
www.doverpublications.com

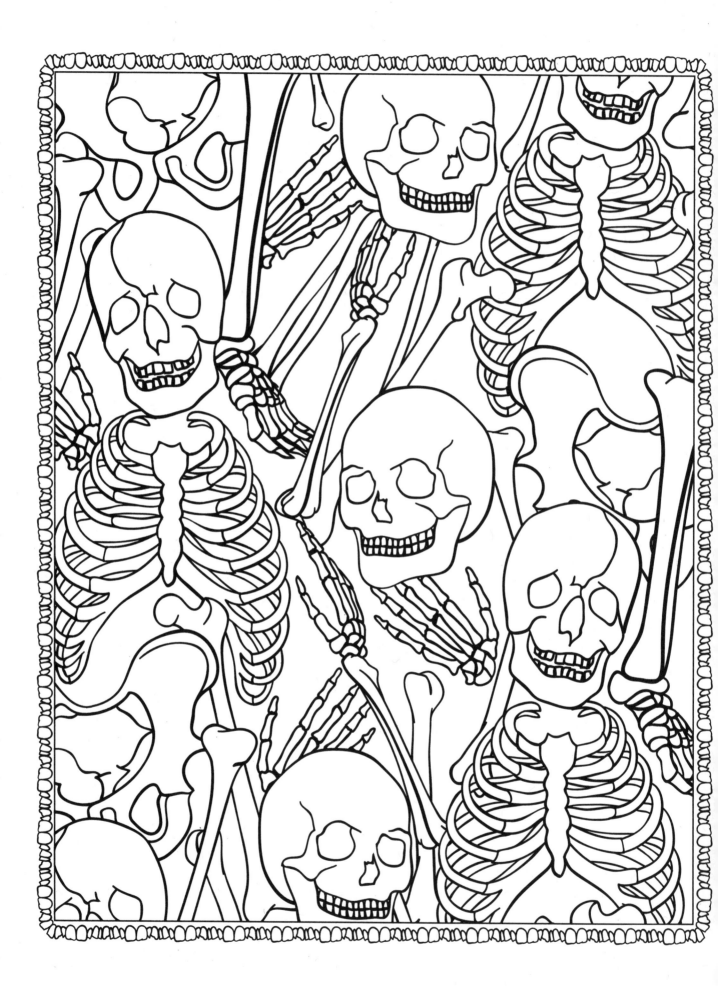

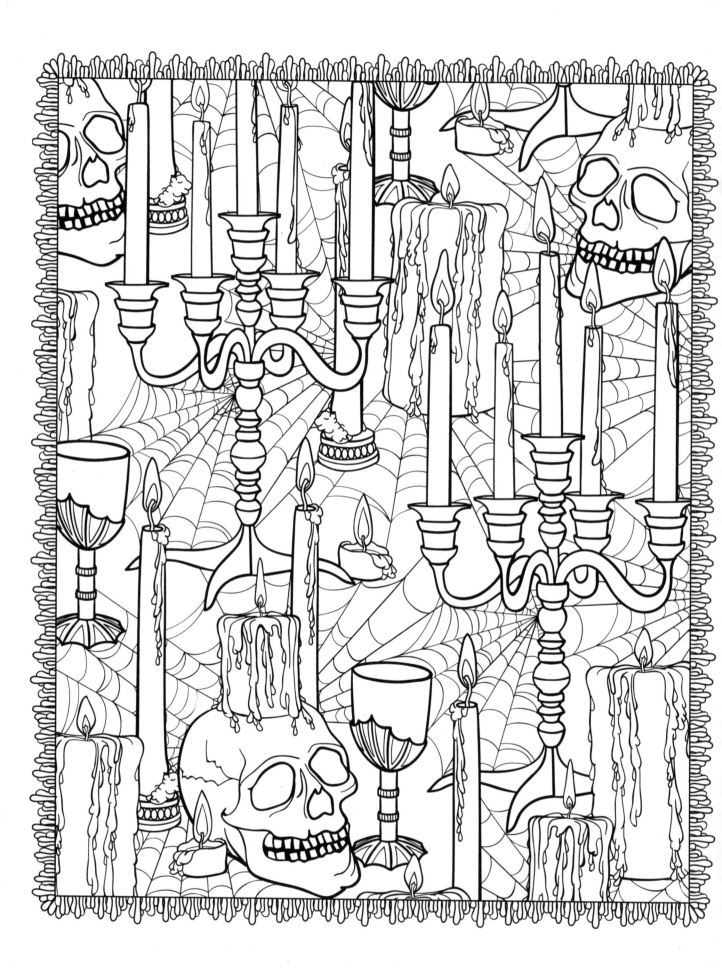

12